Country Kitchen Collection

# Fruit Basket

Balthasar van der Ast (c.1590–c.1656) *Still Life of Cherries and Peaches*

Country Kitchen Collection

# Fruit Basket

Anna Nicholas

Floris van Schooten (fl.1605–1655) *Girl Selling Grapes from a Table with Fruit and Vegetables*

Grange
BOOKS

ACKNOWLEDGEMENTS
All pictures by courtesy of The Bridgeman Art Library.

Preserving Jam by Frederick Daniel Hardy (1826-1911) Boume Gallery, Reigate, Surrey/Bridgeman Art Library, London. Girl Selling Grapes from a Large Table Laden with Fruit and Vegetables by Floris van Schooten (fl.1605-1655) Johnny van Haeften Gallery, London/Bridgeman Art Library, London. Apple Dumplings by George Leslie Dunlop (1835-1921) Hartlepool Museum Service/Bridgeman Art Library, London. Still Life of Cherries and Peaches by Balthasar van der Ast (c.1590-c.1656) Johnny van Haeften Gallery, London/Bridgeman Art Library, London. Figs by Giovanna Garzoni (1600-1670) Galleria Palatina, Florence/Bridgeman Art Library, London. Still Life of Fruit, 17th Century Italian School Rafael Valls Gallery, London/Bridgeman Art Library, London. Lemons in a Blue Basket by Christopher Wood (1901-1930) Walter Hussey Bequest, Pallant House, Chichester/Bridgeman Art Library, London. A Basket of Strawberries on a Stone Ledge by Eloise Harriet Stannard (1829-1915) Christopher Wood Gallery London/ Bridgeman Art Library, London. Still Life of Raspberries, Gooseberries, Peach and Plums on a Mossy Bank by Oliver Clare (fl.1853-1927) Phillips, The International Fine Art Auctioneers/Bridgeman Art Library, London. Still Life by Eloise Harriet Stannard (1829-1915) Ackermann and Johnson /Bridgeman Art Library, London. Woman Carrying Fruit, detail from the Birth of St. John the Baptist (fresco) by Domenico Ghirlandaio (1449-1494) Santa Maria Novella, Florence/Bridgeman Art Library, London. Photo credit: K&B News Foto, Florence. Man and Woman Before a Table Laid with Fruits and Vegetables by Georg Flegel (1563-1638) Private Collection/Bridgeman Art Library, London. Peasant Festival, 1649 by David Ryckaert (1612-61) Kunsthistorisches Museum, Vienna/Bridgeman Art Library, London. A Still Life of Raspberries in a Wicker Basket by William B. Hough (fl.1857-1894) Christopher Wood Gallery, London/ Bridgeman Art Library, London. An Allegory of Summer by Lucas van Valkenborch (c.1535-1597) Johnny van Haeften Gallery, London/ Bridgeman Art Gallery, London. Fruit Market by Lucas van Valkenborch (c.1535-1597) Johnny van Haeften Gallery, London/Bridgeman Art Library, London. An Allegory of Summer by Sebastien Vrancx (1573-1647) Johnny van Haeften Gallery, London/Bridgeman Art Library, London. Sitll Life by Bartholommeo Bimbi (1648-1725) Private Collection/Bridgeman Art Library, London. Tea on the Terrace at St-Maxime by Henri Lebasque (1865-1937) Christie's London/Bridgeman Art Library, London. Woman Peeling Apples (detail) by Gerard Ter Borch (1617-1681) Kunsthistorisches Museum, Vienna/Bridgeman Art Library, London. Interior with Figures and Fruit by David Emil Joseph de Noter (b.1825) Gavin Graham Gallery, London/Bridgeman Art Library, London. La Desserte, 1897 by Henri Matisse (1869-1954) © Succession H. Matisse/Dacs/Bridgeman Art Library, London. The Basket of Fruit by Frans Snyders (1579-1657) Prado, Madrid/Bridgeman Art Library, London. The Orange Gathers by John William Waterhouse (1849-1917) Christie's, London/Bridgeman Art Library, London. Still Life with Apples by Gustave Courbet (1819-1877) National Gallery, London/Bridgeman Art Library, London. A Spilled Bag of Cherries by Antoine Vollon (1819-1900) Johnny van Haeften Gallery, London/Bridgeman Art Library, London. The Cherry Picker by Berthe Morrisot (1841-95) Private Collection/Bridgeman Art Library, London/Giraudon. A Still Life of Peaches, Apples and Grapes in a Wicker Basket, Flowers in a Chinese Vase and Two Parrots on a Table by a follower of Balthasar van der Ast (c.1590-c.1656) Bonhams, London/Bridgeman Art Library, London. Woman Digging in an Orchard by Camille Pissarro (1830-1903) Private Collection/Bridgeman Art Library, London. William Tell's Son by Ford Madox Brown (1821-1893) Forbes Magazine Collection, New York/Bridgeman Art Library, London. Sunny Morning, 1905 by Karoly Ferenczy (1862-1917) Magyar Nemzeti Galeria, Budapest/Bridgeman Art Library, London. Fruitmarket (Summer) 1590 by Frederik Valkenborch (1570-1623) Kunsthistorisches Museum, Vienna/Bridgeman Art Library, London.

The Publishers have made every effort to trace the copyright holders of material reproduced within this compilation. If, however, they have inadvertantly made any error they would be grateful for notification.

Published in 1996
by Grange Books
An imprint of Grange Books Plc.
The Grange
Grange Yard
London SE1 3AG

ISBN 1 85627 729 1

Printed in China

*This book is not intended to be an in-depth look at the technique of cooking: there are a myriad of books which do just this and which go into the nuances of producing many of the dishes described in this volume, most of which have been around for a very long time and exist in many variations even across national boundaries. It is a celebration of food in its wider sense; as an important part of the development of civilized behaviour in which society is bonded together in the acts of eating, discussing and depicting food which is, after all, a prime necessity for our continued existence.*

William B. Hough (fl.1857–1894) *A Still Life of Raspberries in a Wicker Basket*

# Foreword

*'Make use of time, let not advantage slip;*
*Beauty within itself should not be wasted;*
*Fair flowers that are not gathered in their prime,*
*Rot and consume themselves in little time.'*

William Shakespeare (1564–1616) *Venus and Adonis*

Shakespeare's words could also apply to the soft fruits of summer which are with us for so short a span. There was something rather satisfying about the time when we only ate fruits and vegetables in their season, when we eagerly looked forward to the next treat — the first tender peas or succulent raspberrries — as the year progressed along its natural course, month by month. Then, we were more inclined to attempt to capture the essence of summer by laying down a wide range of preserves and chutneys against the leaner winter months.

Now, of course, we are spoiled for choice, there is no such thing as purely seasonal produce and fresh strawberries and peaches are flown in from the other side of the world for us to eat in the depths of winter. Nevertheless, the soft fruits are an all-important part of the summer menu, eaten out-of-doors in a sunlit garden or to the evocative sound of leather on willow or tennis ball on racquet.

Marvellously good for our health, all fruits contain a rich supply of vitamins, minerals and all-important fibre as well as being a delight to the eye and palate. Nowadays, we are advised to eat five pieces of fruit every day and this is a sensible recommendation in order to preserve a healthy heart and protection from disease. This is no hardship: after all, what could be more delicious and refreshing!

Lucas van Valkenborch (c.1535–1597) *An Allegory of Summer*

## Pears on Toast

*As with most good ideas it is the most simple that is often the most effective. This lovely dessert could not be easier to prepare and you are more than likely to have the ingredients already conveniently to hand.*

Peel, core and slice some ripe pears, such as Williams or Comice, sprinkling them as you go with lemon juice to avoid discoloration. Dip slices of soft textured bread such as *brioche* or even day-old regular bread into melted butter. Lay the slices on a baking sheet, sprinkle with castor sugar and arrange the sliced pears on top. Finish with another scattering of sugar and bake in the top of a moderate oven for 40 minute or so until the edges are crisp and the pears soft.

This would be equally delicious made with pitted and halved apricots or ripe peaches.

*A tree is known by its fruit.*

14th century Proverb

8

Lucas van Valkenborch  *The Fruit Market*

9

# Redcurrant and Cherry Preserve

*This is a delicious way to capture the fleeting tastes and scents of summer which will be appreciated all the more in the bleakness of winter to come.*

Put 4lb (4 quarts) of prepared redcurrants into a large glass or ceramic bowl, cover, and microwave them on full power, without water, until the juice is released. Strain without pressing the fruit so that you are left with about half the quantity of clear juice. Take the same amount of pitted cherries, 6lb (12 cups) sugar and 3 glasses of water, and boil gently until a spoonful sets on a cold plate. Add the redcurrant juice, bring to a boil again and it is ready to put in jars. More unusually, the preserve is lovely served with fresh cream as a dessert.

*Raspberry, strawberry, blackberry jam, tell me the name of your young man.*

Old rhyme

Sebastien Vrancx (1573-1647) *An Allegory of Summer*

10

Bartolomeo Bimbi (1648-1725) *Still Life*

## Dried Fruit Compote

The flavour of most fruits appears to intensify when dried, especially if they have been sun-cured. If you have a glut of apples in the autumn it is a simple matter to dry some of them for use later on, especially in mueslis or compotes.

Core and cut the unpeeled apples into rings, after having soaked them in a weak salt solution. Thread on thin poles and suspend them over a heat source, an Aga or solid fuel range, for example.

For a fruit compote, a more exotic miscellany of dried apricots, prunes, figs and raisins is appropriate. Wash the fruit, if necessary, and place in a large bowl. Cover with fresh orange juice – or you could use a mixture of water and rose or orange flower water for a more oriental touch. Cover, and leave to macerate for as long as possible – up to 48 hours. The fruit will be soft and succulent and a wonderful syrup will have developed.

*Preserve to our use the kindly fruits of the earth.*
The Book of Common Prayer

# Peaches Flambéed in Brandy

*Flambéing, as well as imparting an indescribable flavour to a savoury dish, either at the start or finish of its cooking, is also a good way of removing any excess fat from the sauce. This does not, of course, apply to desserts such as crêpes Suzette, but it certainly helps the flavour along. Whether you decide to perform the operation in the privacy of your kitchen or in full view of your guests at table depends on how confident you are feeling at the time.*

Take 6 large, perfect peaches, skinned and left whole. Poach in half a cup of water and 1cup of sugar which have first been dissolved together to make a syrup and to which the zest of 1 orange has been added. When tender, remove the peaches to a shallow serving dish. Stir a teaspoon of arrowroot mixed with a tablespoon of orange juice into the remaining syrup and boil until perfectly clear. Discard rind and add 3 tablespoons of brandy. Cool until lukewarm. Before serving, gently heat a further tablespoonful of brandy in a ladle, set it alight, and pour over the peaches. Bring to the table flaming.

# Crab Meat with Peaches

*Allow one ripe peach per person. The richness of the meat is nicely balanced by the acidity of the fruit.*

Chop the end off each peach to form a lid. Remove the stone and a little of the inside flesh. Mix this with the crab meat bound together with a little cream. Season with salt and a little *paprika*. Pile the mixture back into the peaches and chill until ready to serve.

Henri Lebasque (1865-1937) *Tea on the Terrace at St-Maxime*

# Apple Cake

*This type of cake is most popular in Scandinavia and produces a wonderful moist fruitiness because the raw apples are enclosed and cooked within the cake mixture ensuring that the maximum flavour is retained. It keeps well but is guaranteed to fly off the plate so fast that the problem of keeping it is never likely to arise.*

Core, peel and thinly slice 2 lbs (1$^{1}/_{3}$ quarts) cooking (baking) apples. Gently melt 8 oz (1 cup) butter and 8 oz (1 cup) castor sugar over a very low heat. Allow to cool slightly then gradually add 8 oz (2 cups) flour, stirring thoroughly all the while, and then 2 eggs. Mix in 4 tablespoons of sultanas and spread two-thirds of the mixture into the bottom of a well-greased cake tin. Place half the sliced apples on top of this, sprinkle with powdered cinnamon, ginger, lemon juice and brown sugar. Cover with the remainder of the apples, a handful of chopped nuts and the rest of the cake mix. Bake in a moderate oven for about 1$^{1}/_{2}$ hours, then test with a skewer. Bake a little longer, if necessary.

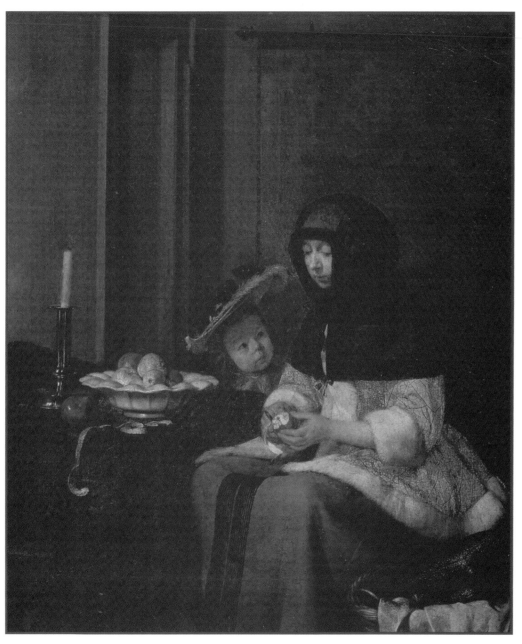

Gerard Ter Borch (1617-1681) *Woman Peeling Apples*

14

*Jehovah created Adam on the sixth day and entrusted him with dominion over all the animals and plants and then he created Eve as a helpmate. In this Eden the humans, plants and animals lived in harmony until Eve made Adam break the order against the eating of fruit from a certain tree. With this breaking of this order of eating, Adam and Eve were expelled from Eden and condemned 'to eat their bread in the sweat of thy face'.*

Genesis 3, 19

Ford Madox Brown (1821-1893) *William Tell's Son*

*Enough is as good as a feast.*

Proverb

15

## Poached Fresh Fruit

*A macédoine of fruits is a visual delight with its intense jewel-like colours, and makes a light and refreshing finish to a substantial meal, especially if it has been full of rich flavours. It is possible to use less than perfect fruits, the kind that you would normally expect to eat in their natural state and at a peak of ripeness. These could be slightly over- or under-ripe but not, of course, completely over the hill.*

Place a few strips of lemon peel together with its juice into a saucepan of water together with 10 fl oz (1¼ cups) water and 2 oz (½ cup) sugar and bring to the boil. Add a mixture of fresh fruits, peeled, pitted and sliced and simmer gently until just tender (15 minutes). You could add a few grapes after the first 10 minutes of cooking time. Remove the fruit carefully, allow it to cool and cover it with the cooking syrup to which you could add a little brandy or fruit liqueur.

David Emil Joseph de Noter (b. 1825) *Interior with Figures and Fruit*

16

Henri Matisse (1869-1954) *La Desserte*

## A Platter of Fresh Fruits

You need do little more than arrange a selection of fruits onto the most beautiful plate that you possess. Fruit is so colourful and has such immediate appeal that you need only cut it up into slices or divide it into segments. Small fruits, such as strawberries, grapes, redcurrants and cherries can be left whole or even frosted with egg white and sugar. It would be wise to dip fruit that is likely to discolour into acidulated water before adding it to your arrangement. Use as many different fruits as possible to create a stunning centre-piece for a summer buffet or picnic.

Frans Snyders (1579-1657) *The Basket of Fruit*

## Melon Sorbet

*A sorbet is the perfect finish to a rich meal and has the advantage of being relatively low in calories. By its very nature a sorbet appears to intensify the flavour of delicate summer fruits and this version is no exception being deliciously and coolly refreshing. Obviously an ice cream maker would make life easier but it is quite possible to make sorbets and granitas – which have an interesting texture with larger crystals – without one.*

*Sorbets, often made from a marc, which is a clear alcohol made from the pressings of grapes after winemaking or other fruits, is often served in France between courses as a way of refreshing the palate and enabling the diner to more easily cope with a large and sumptuous meal.*

Reserving the outer rinds and discarding the seeds, spoon the flesh of 2 medium-sized honeydew or canteloupe melons into a food processor together with the juice of 2 lemons and 8 oz (2 cups) icing or confectioner's sugar. Blend to a smooth purée and turn into an ice cream maker or freezer tray and freeze. Turn into the food processor for a second time and blend again lightly. Put back into the melon skins and re-freeze to use as required.

Melons, as well as fresh figs, are particularly delicious served with wafer-thin slices of Parma ham. It is also worth trying small melons, chilled, halved and de-seeded, their centres filled with a little port, as an interesting if alcoholic start to a meal.

*Hunger is the best sauce.*

Cicero (106-43 B.C.)

19

# Orange Salad

*Combination salads of leaves, vegetables and fruit are enjoying a great popularity at the moment, and justifiedly so. This one would go well as a refreshing side dish for poultry or game birds or as a light hors d'oeuvre.*

*Don't forget how well the flavour of orange goes in other savoury dishes, in the Milanese Ossobuco, in Boeuf à la Bourguignonne and in fish soups, especially the classic Bouillabaisse of Marseille. It has a special affinity with duck and white meats such as pork and chicken.*

Using a serrated knife, cut the skin and white pith from 3 large oranges. Cut them crossways into 6 or 8 pieces over a plate to catch the juices. Place in a salad bowl with thinly sliced red onion rings or sprigs of watercress. Dress with 4 tablespoons of extra virgin olive oil to which 1 teaspoon of wine vinegar and 2 tablespoons of the reserved orange juice has been added together with one teaspoon each of made mustard and sugar. Season with black pepper and salt and garnish with parsley or chives. You could add a final sprinkling of toasted chopped nuts to make this salad even more delicious.

# Duck à L'Orange

Brown an oven-ready duck all over in a large pan on the top of the stove, then flambé it with a little brandy. Return the duck to the oven and surround it with a few chopped carrots, a fresh *bouquet garni* of parsley, thyme and a bay leaf, pepper and salt and a large glass of white wine. Cover and cook in a fairly hot oven for an hour or so or a little longer according to how well done you like your duck. Strain the sauce, which will have formed around the duck, through fine muslin, add the juice and finely chopped zest of an orange and boil for a few minutes. Serve the duck with the sauce poured over and garnished with extra orange slices and sprigs of watercress.

John William Waterhouse (1849-1917) *The Orange Gatherers*

## Cold Cherry Soup

*This is very much an Eastern European dish and is popular in such places as Hungary and Bulgaria. We in the West are somewhat unused to the idea of fruit soups but they are delicious served hot and are even nicer chilled as an interesting start to a summer meal.*

Wash 1½ lb (1¾ quarts) ripe sour cherries. Remove the stones and reserve them. Melt 3 tablespoons of butter in a saucepan. Stir in 1 tablespoon of flour and stir for 1 minute without allowing it to brown. Slowly pour in 2 pints (5 cups) boiling water. Add the cherries, 3 tablespoons sugar, a good splash of kirsch and a piece of lemon peel. Bring to the boil, then simmer for 20 minutes. Meanwhile, add the cherry stones to ½ pint (1 cup) cold water, bringing them to the boil and simmering for 15 minutes. Strain and add to the cherries. This will impart an intriguing almond-like flavour to the soup. Chill well before serving.

If you prefer to serve the soup hot, first line a heated tureen with slices of bread fried in butter and carefully pour the hot soup over.

Antoine Vollon (1833-1900) *A Spilled Bag of Cherries*

22

# Tarte Tatin

*Legend has it that this dish was accidentally invented by the demoiselles Tatin who ran the Hôtel Terminus in Lamotte-Beuvron in the Loire region of France. Apparently, one of the sisters absentmindedly put the apples in the baking tin before she had lined it with pastry. She decided to go ahead and cook it all the same and the result was this famous confection. It is said that the painter Claude Monet paid a visit to the establishment to sample this legendary dish for himself.*

You will need a quantity of sweet shortcrust pastry made in the usual way with 8 oz (2 cups) flour, a pinch of salt, 2 tablespoons of castor sugar, 4 oz (½ cup) butter, 1 egg yolk and a little cold water. This can also be made in a food processor but it is vitally important to roll the dough into a ball, cover it with plastic wrap and chill it thoroughly. Do not attempt to roll it out until the very last minute. For the filling you will need about 3 lb (2 quarts) firm eating apples which have been peeled, cored and quartered. In a heavy skillet or frying-pan, heat 6 tablespoons unsalted butter and when it is melted add 6 oz (1 cup) sugar and stir with a wooden spoon until it takes on a golden hue. Add the apples, sprinkle with lemon juice and cook over a high heat until the apples are tender  and a covering of rich caramel has formed. Transfer to a well-buttered 9-inch (23 cm) loose-based cake tin. Briefly knead the chilled pastry, roll out to an 11-inch (28 cm) circle on a well-floured board. Fold the dough over the rolling pin and cover the apples with it, tucking in the edges between the apples and the edge of the tin. Cut a few holes to allow the steam to escape and bake in a pre-heated oven at 425°F (220°C) for about 30 minutes. Carefully unmould, using a large plate to turn the tart right side (apple side) up.

Gustave Courbet (1819-1877) *Still Life with Apples*

# Fig Roll

*Figs have a strong sensual appeal with their bursting flesh and skins covererd in a light yeast bloom. Their praise has been sung by ancient philosophers and poets alike and the Greeks considered them so beneficial to health that they were included in the diet of the first Olympic athletes. The entire fruit is eaten but they should not be chilled for this dulls their delicious flavour. This dish originated in the South of France and takes only a few minutes to prepare. In this case, however, the fig mixture is lightly chilled which enables it to be neatly and thinly cut before serving.*

In a mortar or blender, crush together 1 lb (2 cups) chopped dried figs with 4 oz (1 cup) blanched, coarsely chopped almonds. Form the mixture into a sausage shape and roll it in icing sugar. Wrap in plastic film and chill for 4 hours. Unwrap, place on a serving dish and slice thinly.
Another way is to bake slightly under-ripe unpeeled figs with a litle water and sugar in the oven and eat them with cream when cold, or they can be made into a conserve – the essence of the Mediterranean caught in a jar.

*Be fruitful, multiply, and replenish the earth.*

Genesis 1, 28

Giovanna Garzoni (1600–1670) *Figs*

Italian School (17th century) *Still Life of Fruit*

26

## Pumpkin Pie

*This dish is always connected with the United States and is regarded as being so American, like the Thanksgiving turkey, that it is almost a national dish.*

You will need sufficient flaky pastry, either bought or made in the usual way, to line a 9-inch (23-cm) flan tin. Either way, it must be well chilled right up to the last minute you need to use it. Halve a 3-lb (1⅓-kg) pumpkin and remove the seeds and strings. Place cut sides down on a baking sheet and bake in a moderate oven until the flesh is soft (1 hour). Remove the cooked pumpkin from the oven and turn up the temperature to 400°F (200°C). Purée the pulp in a sieve or blender and combine ¾ pint (2 cups) of it with 5 oz (½ cup) brown sugar, 1 teaspoon ground cinnamon, a half-teaspoon each of ground ginger and salt and ⅛ teaspoon each of ground nutmeg and cloves. Mix thoroughly and incorporate 12 fl oz (1½ cups) double cream and 3 tablespoons of rum. Line the flan tin with the pastry and pour the mixture into it. Bake for about 45 minutes or until a knife comes out clean when inserted into the pie. Serve either chilled or at room temperature, on its own or topped with lightly whipped cream.

## Pumpkin Soup

*This is not quite the same as the American version but it is an interesting variation all the same and originates from France where it is called Potage de Potiron.*

Remove the skin from a pumpkin weighing about 2 lb (1 kg) and cut it into 3-inch chunks. Cut 3 or 4 ripe tomatoes in half and squeeze out the pips. Cut a large onion into thin slivers and place it with the pumpkin and tomatoes in a heavy casserole. Cover with greaseproof paper and a tightly fitting lid and cook in a moderate oven for about an hour. Pass the entire contents of the casserole through a fine sieve, return to the rinsed-out casserole and add 2 pints (5 cups of milk. Bring to the boil and simmer for a few minutes. Season with pepper, salt and a little sugar and remove from the heat. Place a knob of butter, cut into tiny pieces, in the bottom of a heated soup tureen, add 2 egg yolks, cream them both together and add the soup a little at a time. Serve with a little boiled rice mixed in or a sprinkling of croûtons. To more decorative effect, the soup could be served in the pumpkin shell, perhaps for a Hallowe'en supper.

*In this island there are many spices ... their Highnesses may see that I shall give them all the gold they require, spices also and cotton, mastic and aloes. I think also I have found rhubarb and cinnamon.*

Christopher Columbus, on coming upon the West Indies, 1493

## Real Lemonade

*In these days of heavily carbonated drinks laced with suspect chemicals, it makes a welcome change to have a glass of the real thing. It is simplicity itself to make and its sheer deliciousness will make us ask ourselves why we ever bothered with the mass-produced version.*

With a serrated knife, remove the peel from three or more juicy lemons taking care to remove all the pith. In a large jug, cover the lemon peel with 3 tablespoons of sugar and enough boiling water to cover. Leave a metal spoon in while you do this to avoid cracking the jug. Squeeze the lemons and add the juice. Add cold water to taste. Chill thoroughly before serving.

## Lemon Curd

*This is sometimes known as lemon cheese and is another example of how startlingly superior the home-made version is over what can simply be bought from a shop. Orange curd is made in exactly the same way, substituting orange rind and juice for the lemons.*

You will need 6 oz (1 cup) castor sugar, 4 egg yolks, the grated rind and juice of a large lemon, 2 tablespoons of unsalted butter and 1 egg white. Thoroughly whip the egg yolks together with the white. In a double saucepan or a basin over a pan of hot water, gently melt together the sugar and butter, rind and juice and stir for about 15 minutes until thick. Do not overheat or the eggs will curdle and begin to resemble scrambled eggs. Put into jars and seal well. Lemon curd should be made in small quantities and eaten up fairly quickly as it does not possess the same keeping properties as a jam or preserve. Lemon curd is wonderful in small tartlets or as a filling for a Victoria sponge cake topped, perhaps, with lemon frosting.

Christopher Wood (1901-1930) *Lemons in Blue Basket*

Eloise Harriet Stannard (1829-1915) *A Basket of Strawberries on a Stone Ledge*

30

## Strawberries in Wine

*This is a lovely way of eating strawberries and a sophisticated change from the more popular strawberries and cream or strawberry shortcake, though shortbread biscuits, ratafias or langues de chat could be eaten with them.*

The ideal wine for this dish, especially if it is to be made for a special occasion, would be a genuine Burgundy which has a powerful affinity with strawberries being soft and fruity itself. However, any dark, rich red wine will do. Simply hull the fruit after rinsing it briefly (if you really must) and drain well. Put in a bowl, add castor sugar to taste and cover with the wine. Cover with plastic film, allowing the strawberries to macerate in the refrigerator for an hour or so before serving.

*He who does not mind his belly will hardly mind anything else.*

Samuel Johnson (1709-1784)

## Strawberry Vinegar

*Fruit vinegars are enjoying a great revival of popularity at the moment. They are useful in the preparation of interesting salad dressings and marinades and can be used to enliven sauces to serve with meats, poultry and game dishes. Other soft fruits can be used in much the same way, for example, raspberries and blackcurrants.*

To 1 lb (1 quart) strawberries, add 1 pint of white wine vinegar in a glass or china bowl. Cover with a clean cloth and leave to macerate for 3 or 4 days, stirring occasionally. Strain through a fine sieve and measure the liquid. For each pint, allow 12 oz ($1\frac{1}{2}$ cups) of sugar and bring to the boil in a stainless steel pan. Boil until the sugar has dissolved and for a further 10 minutes or so. Pour into hot bottles and seal.

## Gooseberry Fool

*Light and delicious, this is the perfect summer dessert, the slight tartness of the fruit combining deliciously with the cream.*

Gently cook 1 lb (2 cups) gooseberries with sugar to taste. This can be done in a microwave when no added water is required as the fruit will exude its own juices. When tender, pass the fruit through a fine sieve to remove all the little pips. Whip up ½ pint (1 cup) double cream with a little sugar until it is soft and thick. Fold the gooseberry purée into the cream and serve in 4 individual glasses. Decorate with mint leaves or even edible flowers, such as borage or elderflowers. This is equally as delicious made with strawberries, blueberries, rhubarb, or any other soft fruit for that matter; it would be quite hard to say which is best.

Oliver Clare (c.1853-1927) *A Still Life of Raspberries, Gooseberries, a Peach and Plums on a Mossy Bank*

## Gooseberry Sauce

*This sharp green sauce is the perfect foil to an oily fish such as mackerel and perfectly balances its succulent richness.*

To 1 lb (2 cups) gooseberries, simply add 2-3 tablespoons of water and a tablespoon of sugar. Bring to a boil and simmer until the fruit is just soft and has begun to burst and release its juices. Remove from the heat and beat till smooth. You could add a little more sugar during the cooking process if you prefer a slightly sweeter sauce.

*Cooking is like love. It should be entered into with abandon or not at all.*

Harriet Van Horne

Eloise Harriet Stannard (1829-1915) *Still Life*

## Plum Crumble

*This is a good dish to make if you lack the gentle touch and feather-light pastry is not your strong point. Unsweetened, the crumb-like mixture can be used on savoury dishes or made into a scone topping when it is known as a cobbler — another old-fashioned dish. It is especially good with fruits as the juices seep deliciously into the topping in a way that doesn't seem to happen with pastry.*

Place 2 lb (1 kg) whole washed plums in an oven-proof dish. Sprinkle over a little cinnamon and 6 oz (1 cup) demerara sugar. Cover over with a crumble topping made with 8 oz (2 cups) whole wheat flour, 4 oz (½ cup) softened butter and a little brown sugar mixed together between the fingers until it resembles large breadcrumbs. Bake for 40 minutes at 350°F (180°C) until the top is brown. Gooseberries, blueberries and rhubarb are also delicious given this treatment but in the case of the first two the cinnamon should be omitted.

## Locksmith's Apprentices

*The enormous, succulent Californian prunes are ideal for this dish as they are already tender and need no pre-soaking.*

Carefully remove the stones from 12 prunes and replace them with a whole almond. Make some pastry from 8 oz (2 cups) flour, 2 tablespoons castor sugar, an egg yolk and a pinch of salt, bound together with a little white wine. Roll out thinly and divide into 12 rounds wrapping a prune in each. Bake in a moderate oven on a well buttered baking dish for about 15 minutes. Serve hot rolled in sugar and grated chocolate.

Domenico Ghirlandaio (1449-1494) *Woman Carrying Fruit* (From the Birth of St. John the Baptist, detail of fresco)

*Behold I have given you every plant yielding seed, which is upon the face of the earth, and every tree with seed in its fruit; you shall have them for your food.*

Genesis 1, 29

## Pomegranates

This exotic fruit with its beautiful jewel-like seeds is, of course, delicious eaten as it is or you could mash it into a bowl, sprinkle it with rose water and lemon juice and serve chilled. The fresh seeds can also be sprinkled on salads and combined with sauces for fish. The dried seeds make an interesting addition to hummus and tahina, while pomegranate syrup is much used in Middle-Eastern dishes.

# Apple Dumplings

This is an old English favourite for which you will need 8 oz (225 g) shortcrust pastry, either your own or bought ready-made. Roll out and divide the pastry into four rounds or squares and peel and core the apples. Combine some soft brown sugar, lemon rind and soft butter together and use the mixture to stuff the centres of the apples. Stick a clove into the top of the stuffing and put an apple on each piece of pastry. Draw the pastry up around the apples, sealing the edges with a little milk. Place on a greased baking tray and brush the dumplings over with a little more milk and a sprinkling of castor sugar. Cook in a moderate oven for about half an hour. Serve hot or cold with cream or custard sauce.

*'Coleridge holds that a man cannot have a pure mind who refuses apple dumplings.'*

Charles Lamb (1775-1834)

George Dunlop Leslie (1835-1921) *Apple Dumplings*

Georg Flegel (1563-1638) *Man and Woman Before a Table Laid with Fruits and Vegetables*

38

# Summer Pudding

*This is one of the best loved desserts of all time. The only thing that you must do is to make sure that the outside is saturated with the fruit juices which gives an overall rich, ruby colour to the pudding and guarantees a moist, succulent result. Pound cake can be used as an alternative to bread despite its being not quite authentic.*

Gently cook 1 lb (1 quart) raspberries and half that amount each of redcurrants and blackcurrants, each in separate pans, with sugar to taste. Do not stir too much – you need sufficient juice to escape but not too much. Line a 2 pint (1 litre) pudding basin with crustless white bread sliced lengthways. Make sure there are no gaps. Put in layers of the different fruits until the basin is almost full, reserving the juice and keeping it in a jug in the refrigerator. Cover the top of the basin with more bread and cover with a weighted plate. Allow to stand for 24 hours when the bread should have turned uniformly pink. If there are white patches, add a little more of the juice. Turn out and serve with fresh cream and more of the juice poured over.

## Apricot Tart

*This is one of the great classics and the mainstay of the French pâtisserie where the apricots often repose on a base of crème pâtissière or confectioner's custard. Here is a lighter version.*

Make a sweet pastry with 8 oz (2 cups) flour, 4 oz (½ cup) butter, an egg and a pinch of salt. Knead with a little water and leave to rest for an hour or two. Roll out and line the base of a buttered flan tin pricking it here and there. Bearing in mind that the fruit will shrink while cooking, cram in as many stoned, halved apricots as possible. Cook a few extra apricots in water and sugar, strain and reduce the liquid. Use this to glaze the the tart after it has been baked in a moderate oven for about half an hour or so. A little apricot brandy or kirsch would be a nice addition to the fruit glaze.

Frederik Valckenborch (1570-1623) *Fruitmarket (Summer)*, 1590

Cookery means English
thoughtfulness, French art
and Arabian hospitality: it
means the knowledge of all
the fruits and herbs and
balms and spices: it means
carefulness, inventiveness
and watchfulness.

John Ruskin (1819-1900)

Berthe Morisot (1841-1895) *The Cherry Picker*

## Clafoutis

*This famous dessert comes from the Auvergne in central France and consists of a simple batter in which ripe cherries are cooked.*

Make the batter from 1¼ pints (3 cups) milk, 3 tablespoons of flour, three eggs and a pinch of salt. When smooth, mix in 2 tablespoons of kirsch and a few tablespoons of sugar. Butter a shallow oven dish and pile the pitted cherries in the bottom. Strain over the batter mixture and bake for 50 minutes in a pre-heated oven at 375°F (190°C). Sprinkle with sugar and serve with cream, crème frâiche would be even nicer if you have it.

## Cherry Vodka

*This is known in Russia as Vishnyovka and if made when the Morello cherries are ready, towards the end of July, will be ready to drink the following Christmas.*

You will need about 5 lb (2½ kg) sugar to 6 lb (3 kg) Morello cherries. Stem and stone the cherries and put them in stone or glass jars, with layers of sugar in between, finishing with a layer of sugar on top. Crush 3 dozen or so of the cherry stones, tie them up in muslin bags and place a bag in each jar and cover loosely. Stir the cherries every day until the sugar has dissolved, then stop up firmly and leave in a warm place to ferment. When the cherries have stopped fermenting, top up each with a little vodka and leave for as long as possible. Before serving, strain into bottles through muslin. The fruit is delicious eaten with coffee ice cream.

## Peaches with Redcurrants

*The finished dish will be full of a mouthwatering fragrance and wholly irresistible to eat.*

Poach whole ripe peaches in water, with sugar to taste, until tender. Remove the skins and place the peaches on individual serving dishes. Meanwhile, cook 1 lb (1 quart) redcurrants without water but with 4 oz ($^1/_2$ cup) sugar, very briefly in the microwave oven in a covered dish. Remove, strain and chill. Use this purée as a pouring sauce for the peaches. You will find that the flavours of the two fruits combine excellently together. Serve with vanilla ice cream.

## Grapes

*The fruit of the vine is God's special gift to mankind and wine has been made and enjoyed from time immemorial.*

Besides enjoying them in their most magical form – as a delicious wine, the grapes themselves can be served in a number of interesting ways. They go well with fish – think of *Sole Véronique*, rolled fillets lightly poached in white wine and garnished with white muscats. They make a refreshing end to a meal served with a piece of Gruyère: why not serve them as the Italians do in small bunches floating in a bowl of iced water surrounded by ice cubes.

A follower of Balthasar van der Ast c.1590–c.1656) *A Still Life of Peaches, Apples and Grapes in a Wicker Basket, Flowers in a Chinese Vase and Two Parrots on a Table*

*An apple a day keeps the
doctor away.*

Proverb

Camille Pissarro (1830-1903) *Woman Digging in an Orchard*

## Pears in Cider

*You would expect apples to be entirely compatible with their by-product but pears, their more temperamental relations, have an unexpected affinity with cider, too, just as they have with red wine. In Italy they are often stuffed with a mixture of ground almonds and crystallized fruits and baked in Marsala, the famous wine of Sicily, which is also used to enhance sauces for veal and chicken livers. Poached pears are also good with chocolate as anyone who has tasted the dish Poires Belle Hélène will confirm.*

Peel 6 large, unripe pears, following the contours of the fruit and leaving the stems intact. Place in a large ovenproof dish or casserole – there must be enough room to hold the pears comfortably. In a small saucepan, combine 1 pint (2 cups) dry cider with 4 oz ($^{1}/_{2}$ cup) sugar and 2 whole cinnamon sticks and a few cloves. Bring to the boil and pour the liquid over the pears. Cover the casserole and bake in a very slow oven for about 3 hours, basting from time to time. At the end of the cooking time the liquid, if necessary, can be thickened with a little arrowroot mixed with water, and then brought back to the boil. The pears should be well chilled before serving with cream or thick Greek yogurt. This dish can also be made using red wine instead of cider when the pears will develop a most attractive pink colour.

## Imperial/Metric Conversion

### Weights

| | |
|---|---|
| 2 oz | 50 g |
| 2½ oz | 60 g |
| 3 oz | 75 g |
| 4 oz | 110 g |
| 4½ oz | 125 g |
| 5 oz | 150 g |
| 6 oz | 175 g |
| 7 oz | 200 g |
| 8 oz | 225 g |
| 9 oz | 250 g |
| 10 oz | 275 g |
| 12 oz | 350 g |
| 1 lb | 450 g |
| 1½ lb | 700 g |
| 2 lb | 900 g |
| 3 lb | 1.3 kg |

### Volume

| | |
|---|---|
| 5 fl oz (¼ pt) | 150 ml |
| 10 fl oz (½ pt) | 275 ml |
| 15 fl oz (¾ pt) | 425 ml |
| 1 pint | 570 ml |
| 1¼ pints | 725 ml |
| 1¾ pints | 1 litre |
| 2 pints | 1.2 litres |
| 2½ pints | 1.5 litres |
| 4 pints | 2.25 litres |

## Index

Karoly Ferenczy (1862-1917) *Sunny Morning*